PLANETS IN OUR SOLAR SYSTEM

Learn About MERCURY!

BY NATALIE HUMPHREY

Enslow PUBLISHING

DISCOVER!

Please visit our website, www.enslow.com. For a free color catalog of all our high-quality books, call toll free 1-800-398-2504 or fax 1-877-980-4454.

Cataloging-in-Publication Data

Names: Humphrey, Natalie.
Title: Learn about Mercury! / Natalie Humphrey.
Description: New York : Enslow Publishing, 2024. | Series: Planets in our solar system | Includes index.
Identifiers: ISBN 9781978533585 (pbk.) | ISBN 9781978533592 (library bound) | ISBN 9781978533608 (ebook)
Subjects: LCSH: Mercury (Planet)–Juvenile literature.
Classification: LCC QB611.H857 2024 | DDC 523.41–dc23

Portions of this work were originally authored by Daisy Allyn and published as *Mercury: The Iron Planet*. All new material in this edition authored by Natalie Humphrey.

Published in 2024 by
Enslow Publishing
2544 Clinton Street
Buffalo, NY 14224

Designer: Andrea Davison-Bartolotta
Editor: Natalie Humphrey

Photo credits: Cover (Mercury), p. 1 (Mercury) Nerthuz/Shutterstock.com; cover (top), p. 1 (top), series art (backgrounds) Jurik Peter/Shutterstock.com; series art (lens flare) andruxevich/Shutterstock.com; p. 4 Natee Jitthammachai/Shutterstock.com; p. 5 24K-Production/Shutterstock.com; p. 7 Vector Tradition/Shutterstock.com; p. 9 buradaki/Shutterstock.com; p. 11 shooarts/Shutterstock.com; p. 13 NASA/Bill Ingalls; p. 15 NASA, JHU APL, CIW; pp. 17, 19 Vadim Sadovski/Shutterstock.com; p. 21 courtesy of NASA.

Printed in the United States of America

CPSIA compliance information: Batch #CS24ENS: For further information contact Enslow Publishing, at 1-800-398-2504.

CONTENTS

Speeding AROUND

Mercury is not only the smallest planet in our **solar system**. It's one of the fastest planets too! But that's not the only thing that makes Mercury so different from other planets. There's a lot to learn about the closest planet to the sun!

Mercury is around 30,000,000 miles (58,000,000 km) from the sun.

The Shortest YEAR

Mercury has the fastest **orbit** in our solar system. It only takes Mercury 88 days to travel completely around the sun. This is one year for Mercury. But Mercury doesn't spin quickly. One full spin takes 59 Earth days!

Mercury moves around the sun at 29 miles (47 km) per second.

Solar DAY

One **cycle** of day and night, from **noon** to noon, is a solar day. Because of how slow it spins and how fast it orbits, Mercury doesn't have a solar day like Earth. Instead, it takes around 176 Earth days for Mercury to have one solar day!

On its sunniest side, Mercury can reach up to 800°F (427°C).

Missing SEASONS

Mercury doesn't have seasons. Seasons are caused by a planet's **tilt**. As planets move around the sun, different areas receive direct sunlight due to the planet's tilt. This makes areas of a planet hotter or colder. Unlike most planets, Mercury isn't tilted enough to have seasons!

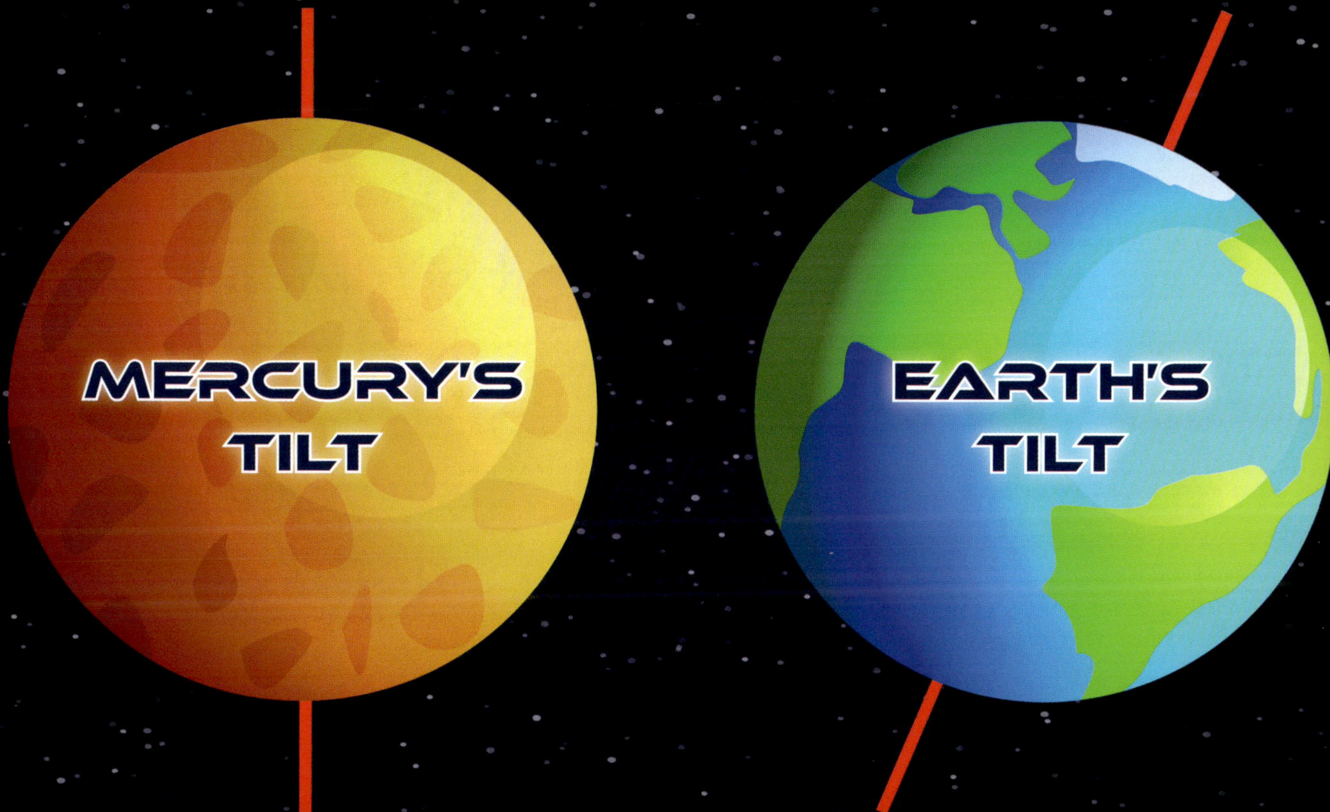

Mercury is only tilted 2 degrees.

MOONLESS

Unlike many of the other planets, Mercury does not have any moons orbiting around it. **Scientists** believe this is because Mercury orbits too close to the sun. Mercury is also so small, its **gravity** isn't strong enough to keep a moon!

Even though Mercury is the closest to the sun, Venus is the hottest planet!

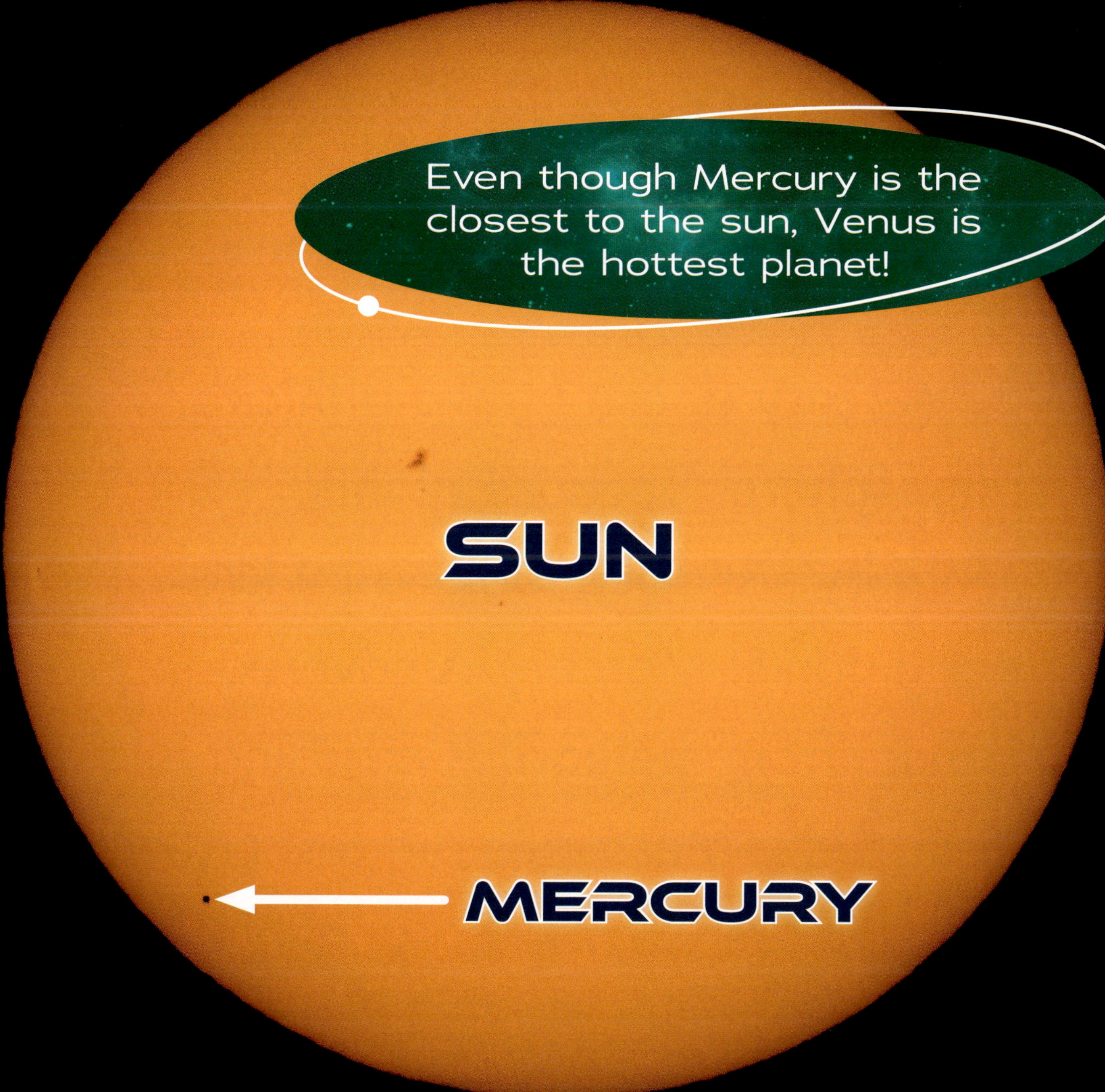

Many CRATERS

Mercury doesn't have a thick **atmosphere**. Because of this, Mercury's surface looks a lot like our moon's! Mercury is covered in **craters** from **meteorites** crashing into its surface. Mercury's biggest crater is called the Caloris Basin and is about 810 miles (1,300 km) wide!

Meteorites often burn up as meteors before hitting planets with thicker atmospheres.

Layered PLANET

Mercury is made of layers just like other planets. Mercury's top layer is called the crust. Below the crust is a rocky layer called the mantle. The inside of Mercury is called the core. The core is made out of thick iron.

Mercury's core is thicker than Earth's.

Tough TARGET

Mercury is very hard for scientists to study! This is because it's very close to the sun. The sun is so hot, it can burn up spacecraft that get too close. The sun's gravity is also so strong, it pulls in anything that gets too close.

Many space **probes** can't spot Mercury past the sun.

Exploring MERCURY

Two space probes have seen Mercury. The Mariner 10 was the first probe to see Mercury up close. The second, the MESSENGER probe, orbited around Mercury. Both probes helped us learn much more about Mercury. Who knows what we could learn next!

MESSENGER PROBE

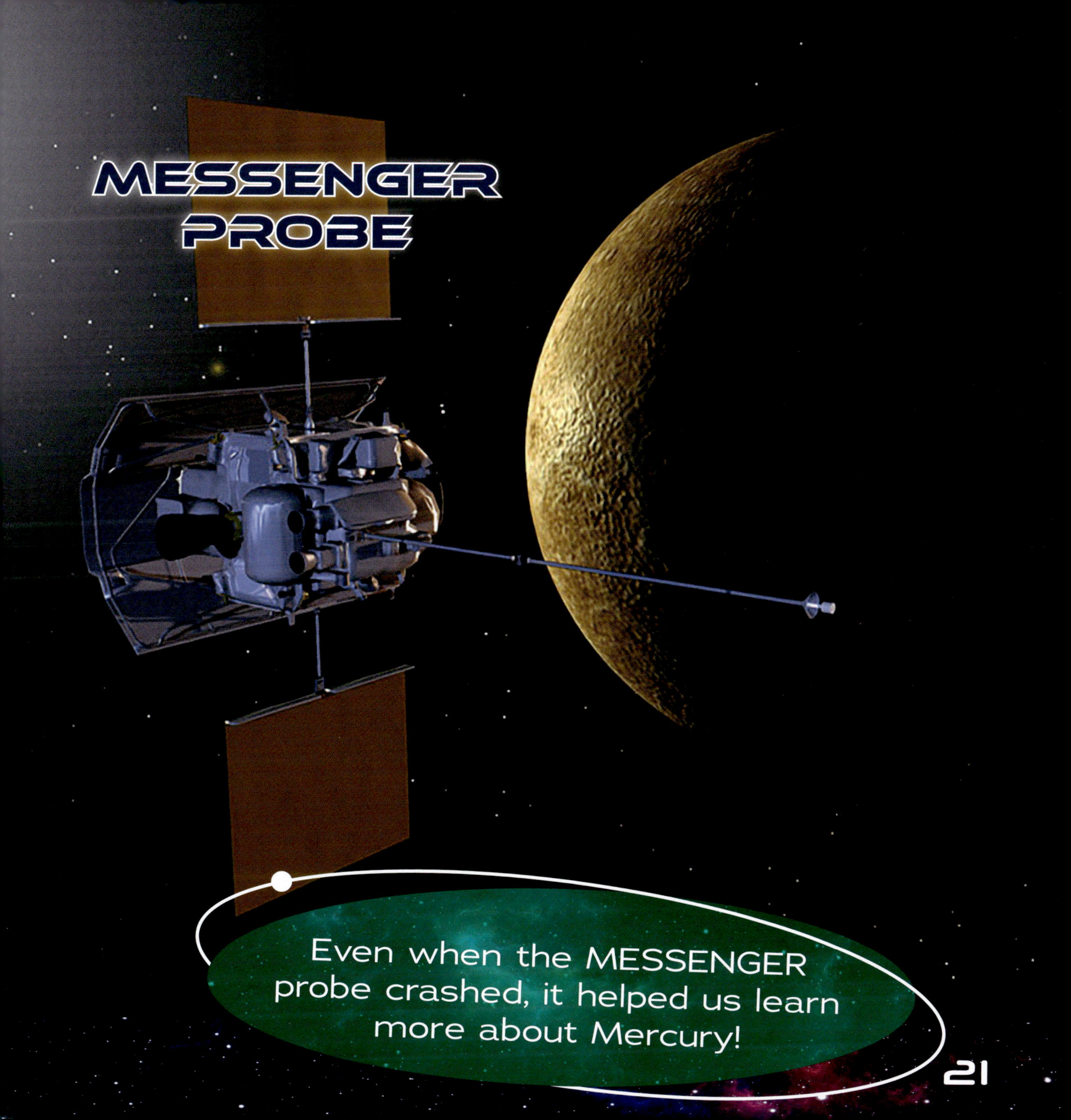

Even when the MESSENGER probe crashed, it helped us learn more about Mercury!

WORDS TO KNOW

atmosphere: The mixture of gases that surround a planet.

crater: A bowl-shaped hole on the surface of a planet or moon.

cycle: A sequence of events that repeats.

gravity: The force that pulls objects toward the center of a planet or star.

meteorite: A space rock that has reached a planet's surface.

noon: In terms of solar time, when the sun is highest in the sky.

orbit: To travel in a circle or oval around something.

probe: An unmanned spaceship.

scientist: Someone who studies the way things work and the way things are.

solar system: The sun and all the space objects that orbit it, including the planets and their moons.

tilt: Slanted, not straight up and down.

FOR MORE INFORMATION

BOOKS

Koestler-Grack. *Curious About Mercury*. Mankato, MN: Amicus/Amicus Ink, 2022.

Storm, Marysa. *Mercury*. Mankato, MN: Black Rabbit Books, 2023.

WEBSITES

NASA Space Place

spaceplace.nasa.gov/all-about-mercury/en/

Learn more about Mercury and what we've discovered so far from NASA!

National Geographic Kids

kids.nationalgeographic.com/space/article/mission-to-mercury

Check out interesting videos, fun facts, and more about Mercury!

INDEX